MW00413619

Tracy Rittmueller immerses us in a forest of imagery, encouraging us to consider the small details of nature as well as its grandeur, and illuminating the ferocity and complexity of the pursuit of grace and harmony.

   –Kris Bigalk, author of *Enough,* (NYC Books, 2018)

Tracy Rittmueller's lyrical poems inhabit a many-roomed mansion of emotions. There are small-windowed rooms filled with grief and loss, other rooms filled with beauty and wonder, and still others that are bright with a soothing, healing light. You'll enjoy a stroll through this mansion of poetry, and as you do, you'll experience what it is to be truly human.

   –Bill Meissner, author of five books of poetry and 2 novels, including *Summer of Rain, Summer of Fire*

Still Life Broken and Repaired by Tracy Rittmueller is a moving exploration of the pain dementia causes as it burrows into a loving relationship. In these arresting poems, the speaker grapples with her partner's dementia and its ensuing uncertainties and injustices—the loss of work, of memory, of romantic connection, and of a dreamed-of future. Rittmueller's honest and vulnerable poems explore the gray ravages of sadness, but they also burst with colorful dragonflies, wild lupine, deep forests, and days spent harvesting carrots. Nature offers a much-needed diversion from ongoing loss, and it provides reminders that love came first, and love remains. In the poem "Learning Kintsugi" (the Japanese art of repairing breaks in pottery with gold), Rittmueller writes, "because the art / of golden repair is the art of refusing / to hide the beautiful strength of our damage" (39). Quiet despair commingled with a desire for hope carves a path through grief in this powerful, must-read collection.

> **—Paige Riehl,** author of *Suspension* (Terrapin Books, 2018)

Still Life, Broken and Repaired is a work that starts in the key of grief and plays – sometimes desperately, sometimes joyously – until it modulates into the sound of hope.

    –Dennis Vogen, author of the graphic novel series *Brushfire*

In *Still Life, Broken and Repaired*, Tracy Rittmueller explores the "blemished catalogue of blossoming contentments" that is life with her beloved. "Because poems are the ghosts/of stories too fragile to be spoken," this small, fierce, and beautiful book calls on Hesse, Rilke, and Rumi as Rittmueller grapples with what it means to live with and love someone whose mind is diminishing. The author strikes a delicate balance here, drawing strength and inspiration from nature and art, while leaving the reader with admiration for the poet's quiet power, and wonder for the couple's abiding love.

    –KateLynn Hibbard, author of *Simples* (Howling Bird Press , 2018)

Still Life, Broken and Repaired

Also by Tracy Rittmueller

Relearning the Lullaby

Still Life, Broken and Repaired

Tracy Rittmueller

LYRICALITY PRESS

© 2023 by Tracy Rittmueller

Lyricality Press
P.O. Box 172
Sauk Rapids, MN 56379

https://lyricality.org

Published 2023 by Lyricality Press
Printed in the United States of America
Cover art and design by Lily Brutger
The text of this book is set in Apple Chalkduster and Avenir Next

ISBN: 978-0-9655922-4-6

for Kenneth Allen Karner Rittmueller

in loving memory of Patricia Fargnoli (1937-2021)
NH Poet Laureate 2006-2009

Still Life, Broken and Repaired

ii.

iii.

Introduction

In that liminal space between past and future, the present can be a moment of intense realization. This is not always an easy lesson, and never is this more apparent than in this collection of poems by Tracy Rittmueller. In this brilliant work of the heart, we begin by reflecting on the past's joyful innocence. In "Sonnet to Negotiate Peace with Your Dementia," the speaker writes: "I thought I might explain why we're broken. / But sleep. This, too, will remain unspoken." This poem opens Part I with the sure knowledge that nothing remains the same even while holding tight to the past. Acceptance is elusive, as another poem, "Pain by Number," shows so well. The speaker has come to understand that her love has dementia, but has decided to celebrate what was, because the other option—to accept the full weight of her grief in the present moment—is still too painful. As an editor, most of the poems that appear in my inbox every day deal with grief and love, yet few manage to walk the border of both with such grace and lightness as does this book of poetry.

In Part II, reality becomes more apparent and therefore more painful. The speaker turns toward beauty in the face of overwhelming knowledge in "Nightfall, with Perfumed Air," a fitting opening poem for the middle section. The struggle to accept what must be is further highlighted in "That Saturday Late Autumn." The choice to believe in love and continue forward is explored in all of its messy, painful tragedy as the poems continue. Yet, it is only in Part III that this collection truly illuminates the breath-stealing intensity of dementia. "Resolution at the Height of Breath" presents this experience in stark terms, as a choice that happens in the midst of it all. The poem's clear imagery and onomatopoeia draw the reader inside this reality, teaching that all one can do is live in the present. In this poem, I'm reminded of Auden's words in "Musée des Beaux Arts," where suffering takes place while ordinary life continues. In Rittmueller's poem, likewise, the lilacs bloom and birds joyously broadcast vibrance from every direction right into the center of the speaker's devastation.

The poems in the Part III also physically fracture in shape and size as the inevitable progression of loss steals into the imagery. In these poems, though the speaker is poised between joy and grief, every moment is a choice toward understanding and acceptance. In "Dragonflies Wed in the Air," there is a celebration of fragile persistence. At the end of the poem, the speaker tricks fear with this diversion of attention in order to pursue gratitude even as her lover's "mind is memory-mangled." Even more fracturing happens in "After Survival / Our Souls Remember" as the speaker in the poem wrestles with fear yet again. Each image is a piece of the whole, but unable to reside comfortably in order, the staggered lines illustrate the disintegration of the present into the future.

At its core, this collection is a shout out to the universe about persistence. About love and beauty. Images of the cosmos and the ocean (both overwhelming spaces) coexist in time and place with fear, loss, and grief. The speaker grapples with the minutiae of dementia in everyday life with a hand outstretched to the beauty that surrounds us. How can such dissimilar things coexist? That is the question these poems answer. The conclusion is not simple.

In the penultimate poem, "Learning Kintsugi," the construction of beauty from a fractured item presents the ultimate allegory. The broken object is the speaker's life and the repair is both necessary and illuminating. This poem informs the collection's title. As one reads through this book, the splintered pieces of poems are glued together with lush imagery and difficult realizations, until at the end, "the art / of golden repair is the art of refusing / to hide the beautiful strength of our damage." The speaker has learned to gild pain with beauty. The reader has learned that beauty in loss is indeed possible.

—**Christine Klocek-Lim**, editor of Autumn Sky Poetry DAILY

i.

And if the first duty of the spirit is leaping joy,
and the second
the slow stroll of serenity,

then grief, the third, comes bending on his walking stick,
holding a trowel to dig where the loves have gone

—Patricia Fargnoli
"Duties of the Spirit"

Sonnet To Negotiate Peace With Your Dementia

You're dozing in your rocker, feet planted.
You clutch the chair's arms, appearing prepared
for the shock of bad news, your neck slanted
head jutting forward. Oh my dear gray scared
bird, while invisible worms still burrow
you stop searching for a table to hold
your reading glasses. And then you furrow
your forehead, begin to snore. You turn old.
The unread want ads lie on your stomach.
They rise and fall between us as we breathe.
Will I tell you? No, I'd rather mimic
you now, observe in silence all that seethes.
I thought I might explain why we're broken.
But sleep. This, too, will remain unspoken.

This Ambiguous Grief's Stunning Questions

sound like howling beasts or mourning ghosts
as if nature knows all that moves through and away
is carried on stricken tones

                                     smells piney
as a breath taken in bitter cold and held
gingerly like a child's hand then unavoidably

                                 released
how will we abide

                                 the blinding sting
of knowing not only you but even your

                                       voice will leave us?
seems this intends to hollow us out

                                 to form

                                       depressions
as if now there must be made basins

                                 within us
to contain
something

                                 but what will remain
of us?

Pain By Number

*"On a scale of 1-10, with one being
no pain at all and 10 being the worst pain imaginable,
how would you rate your pain?"*

1. For rest and for raging.
My lark nest. My meadow.

2. Inferior chocolate
and sickly-sweet cherries.

3. Timidity in bone
bandaged in damaged skin.

4. Lair, lap and wound
signal, beat and breath.

5. My momentary tomb
cocoon, cave and tome.

6. Humming to allay
sensation, an ocean.

7. Under the bed with
reasons not to sleep.

8.   Bellowing wolves
after my carriage.

9.   Clutching my children;
the driver would toss them.

10.   Tricked, wrecked, a pawn
burning blind and shushed.

Backlit Encounter

after "Barn Silhouette," photograph by Cheryl Winter

Whatever stands between the viewer
and the source of light is silhouetted
without depth. With sharpened form
and enhanced negative space
perspective will be lost.
The world is full of grieving hearts.
This could be the beginning of winter.

It might also be early spring. The sun's glare
captured in its ritualistic east to west
race could be setting. It might also be
ascending. We have no way of knowing
whether to pay attention to this tree
and this barn and their lack of three-
dimensionality or whether to study

the white hot glow at the coral horizon
and those mares' tail clouds flicking
the pallid sky. It is exactly our loss
of confidence that causes us to pause
not merely to ask but also to open
our eyes to the air and to everything
that exists between us, present but invisible

as love when we are too wounded to speak.
This breeze smells like apple cider vinegar
but tastes like frost. Our stopping
to examine this moment is more than
we could have expected. It might even be
sacramental. And now do you remember
how we came to be who we are?

Hunting For A Way Through

after that unexpected thaw it turned cold again of course
deep snow reformed into a sheet the color of fog
it could support the weight of a husband and wife
for days it remained cloudy / the world appeared cemented
then came that hazy morning when a fox emerged in the dim

\ opening /

hearing a whisper of motion the hungry thing shot up
like a geyser and stiffened her legs into spears
falling back to earth \ such eager paws
might splinter the crusted snow to reveal something

/ satisfying \

only instead of breaking through / this fox ricocheted
she tried again of course and after many weakening attempts
to get below the surface \ the sorry creature limped away
defeated for now and now this unpunctuated poem will
not let me make it the end of the story about these
melting and solidifying contentions | threatening to best us

For Rest And For Raging

an improvisation on Rainer Maria Rilke's Sonnets to Orpheus (1)

Breath, you invisible poem,
continuance in and around my being,
circling the pure, transposing cosmos. Balance
where rhythmically I transpire.

You are the singular wave, whose
gradually changing ocean I am;
you are the subject of all possible oceans—
Expansion.

How many of your destinations existed
within me? Some exhalations
leave home like my son.

Do you know me, air, when you return,
you, my slippery cover,
the greening surround of words?

When She Stitched The Flag

It was more like this, I imagine:

She waited too long for word from the son
who had marched off with the easy optimism
of men concerned only with ideas.
A low tone sounded in her soul; she knew he was dead.
And the howl that can never be voiced
worked its way through her blood to her fingers.
She selected muslin from his christening gown,

blue from the dress she wore when
his father courted her, and then
something red. She sat on her porch rocking
and stitching and humming to herself
(the neighbors thought) but it was no tune;
it was the mourning voice that knows no language.

My grandmothers taught me the value of stitching,
piecing scraps into blankets. Sometimes
the waiting days are so endless,
tears so familiar they are meaningless.
There is simply nothing else to do.

So you carefully select the fabric,
thread the needle, place the thimble on
the third finger of your hand and
you make something.

ii.

lady i swear by all the flowers. Don't cry
—the best gesture of my brain is less than
your eyelids' flutter which says

we are for each other;…

—E.E. Cummings
"since feeling is first"

Nightfall, With Perfumed Air

From outside the forest I look in
past lichened trunks with splayed branches
past pine boughs dark with evening
past shadows' beckoning eyes.
The clouds drift east toward promised dawn.

They hasten like children toward candlelight.
They retreat like memories of crimson peonies.
They wear blue and gray garments, spun of air
and droplets of mercy. A yellow shaft
slants across the ridge before it, too, departs.

I finger our future farewell. Its fringe
switches my skin—brief sensation—
and then my dread hangs like willow boughs
breathless as the clouds drift east
as if resolved to go where you are not.

Hush, I tell my own mind now. Wait.
In perfect trust a doe and her fawn
step out from the forest. The doe is alert.
The fawn reclines into the hillside like a child
into its mother. I have seen this, I have seen this twice:

how together at nightfall they come
to this place white with flowers,
how the doe knows death, how the fawn knows not
yet they come because here is where the clover grows
and here is where nightfall tastes sweet.

So Now We Lose All Track Of Time

In times of plenty you brought magenta
and gold astralomeria.
> Bouquets of yellow tulips' stems curved
> swanlike over the edges of vases.

Then after your impairment you could no longer work,
you worried about money
> and still you would surprise me
> with a single white rose.

During this your slow departure, when I consider this
withering   loss of you,
> these Minnesota prairie wildflowers and vast skies
> like shifting blue rivers white with rapids,

these dawn clouds like mountains tinged pink
delight me and I lose myself.

> Is this what it's like when you lose all
> track of time?

I think what I was trying to say when sadness crept in
to ravage me is that my fascination
> with horizons (whenever I feel shipwrecked)
is a kind of iconography, an attempt to classify
> incomprehensible beauty.

So now we are traveling while standing still,
                    we live backward while memorizing
this blemished catalogue of blossoming contentments.

That Saturday Late Autumn

we woke chilled that morning
we pulled every carrot from the garden
dug the gladioli
spread their bulbs
to dry in the weakening sun
you wore that plaid shirt
its pockets frayed
its cuffs
thinned from years of washing
skimmed your swelling knuckles
your fingers stiffened
you never complained
for an hour or so you sat silent there
mentioning nothing
about how much work remained
how little time
we drank tea
you built a birch bright fire
washed all those carrots
the peeler skinning them with a whisper
of some unfathomable wisdom
and the wood stove simpered and clicked
while all the rooms grew warmer

But Would I Still Desire To Plant

with you in that spring garden again?
Its gate remained open all April.
Orderly rows of shoots emerged.
Vines surged toward the sun and we
who thought we knew so much, misjudged
when the rain would come. Then overhead
blue-green swallows' romance became
a chattered warning before the storm
hollowed trees into vessels sky
would pour itself into. A sudden
seepage of heat spiraled up while
currents rearranged those branches
hiding an Evening Grosbeak.
The humid space between us shrank
as we ran cold and sodden, whooping
together through spinning light, through mist
rising. Inside the house we stripped
to inspect each other for ticks. Of course
we knew we were naked. We enjoyed
our bodies. It never occurred to me
that one day you'd see me differently,
as if through squall-drenched windows.
Now I reimagine how we
can grow intimacy in this
stunning chaos of your mind altered.

Nothing prepared me for this, although
I might have recognized the truth
that late autumn evening later
that year, after our harvest of carrots—
how little time remained for us before
your mind would begin its slowdown.
Never did I think that one day
looking back I would ask myself,
would I still have desired to plant
with you, had I known our lives would
come to this unknowing?

Fidelity After Dementia

Remember years ago, that man in Tennessee?
We were on a bus gadding around like tourists.
He was on his way to Walmart to look for work,
he said. His sun-cragged face, his blond hair slightly
graying. He appeared near forty. His jeans were clean,
his white shirt's cuffs only slightly frayed, but who gives
a job to a guy with pink-rimmed eyes and trembling hands?
So we asked him to join us for tortillas, rice and beans.
He accepted then bowed his head and wept, repeating
so softly we hardly heard: *God is good. God is so good to me.*
What that man needed more than a meal was to tell someone
his story. We learned where he slept—in a tent
in the woods. And where he bathed—the Stones River.
Early one morning, he woke to find a skunk on his
feet. Hours he lay awake and still as death until the critter,
who was only after all seeking some warmth, moseyed
away. These days, when someone says that *God is good,*
my throat can ache as if I've swallowed alabaster shards.

Have I squandered all my treasured hope on bankrupt fables?
How will we endure this loss when the stories we shared
were like doves, when the very air was lit with mercy?
So we trust it must be true that love will never fail.

Then come those inevitable days when the whole world reeks of moldy leather. My untested conviction vanishes like a flame extinguished and at the same time I remember— because I am conjoined to your mind even in its decline, I am witness to this transformation of gem to star to glare in the womb of your brain. And often enough I sense an inviolable presence—your essence—and so I remain.

Regarding An April
an improvisation on Rainer Maria Rilke's "aus einem April"

Once more the forest is fragrant.
Larks hover, then rise,
lifting the sky that weighed
heavy on your shoulders;
true, through branches you saw
how empty it all was,
but after many rainy afternoons
came those brand-new
sun-burnished hours flying
reverently, grazing
bruised windows with their wings.

Then all grew silent. Even rain slipped
more quietly, darkening the stones' sheen
while sound crouched calmly down
to witness forsythias' breaking buds.

Healing Is A Never Ending Departure
an improvisation after "Stufen" by Hermann Hesse

Like every flower fades and every childhood
withers into age, every stage
of life blooms; each insight, too.
And every goodness blossoms in its time
yet will not last forever. In every purpose,
in every call of life, the heart
must willingly let go.
                                And then begin again,
that with fortitude, yet not without some lamentation,
we may give ourselves to new endeavors.
So let us dare to journey
from provision to provision.
Let's cling to no familiar thing as if to home,
for we are scarcely settled in our cozy way of life
when fear will rear to threaten
our tranquil disposition. To be free
of a grasping, acquisitive nature we must
be ever ready to depart, to travel on.
Perhaps even the hour of our death
will be like another eviction,
renewing our vigor. Life calls us
to our never ending story.
All is still well.
Take heart, dear heart.
Release, that you may heal.

What Is There About Us Always (i)

You gave me a teacup, terra-cotta inside, outside
        sun-washed like some villas in Italy.
It pleased me, as it pleases me when
        every morning you wake early
to prepare my tea, even now when you cannot remember
        the day, washing dishes I knocked my teacup
against the faucet. *My teacup*. I gathered
        ochre shards, trashed them on the day's spent tea
leaves, said nothing. Finding those fragments
        you spoke one word. *Oh*. Rinsed them,
dried them, glued them together. Later
        you brought home a miniature cactus
encircled with thorns. You potted
        potentially maiming barbs, tamed them
in that teacup, fragile as the distinction between scars
        and art. Sometimes I worry your tenuous
memory will fracture our companionship.
        But I know who you are, always the one
who salvaged those wrecked remnants—
        my heart—to restore that broken vessel—me.

iii.

we are for each other; then
laugh, leaning back in my arms
for life's not a paragraph

And death i think is no parenthesis

–E.E. Cummings
"since feeling is first"

Incantation to Conjure Courage
an improvisation on Rainer Maria Rilke's
"Ich lebe mein Leben in wachsenden Ringen"

We live our lives in billowing spheres
arching and aching over everything.
Maybe we won't reach the last circle
but we will die trying.

We circle God, spiraling the ancient
tower, revolving for thousands of years.
And we still don't know: are we kestrels or storms?
Or are we the first oceans' singing?

In A Cove In The Yorks, Maine, I Dare To Hope Again

Where the ocean heaves itself to shore
    my every thought pitches to the surface
and too many memories submerged
    in decades of unspoken fear roil up and under,

while from millions of miles away, light formed
    of particles billions of eons old arrives
to gleam in rising tide. Inside the waves,
    as if water possesses a soul, a lustrous

glow shows itself metallic, then curls under
    and back to the depths: images of stars
and planets, residue of cosmic chorus,
    bubble gum comics, iron pipes oxidized

and barnacled, bits of brick, fragmented
    cargo from centuries-old sunken ships,
a stone from an ancient oceanic
    volcano. So much approaches us without

our notice. If I found an early reader washed of words,
    opening its baptized content would be as precious
as reclaiming my own disowned emotions. Both
    silence and *feeling* are authentic responses

to purity, as well as to injustice. Movingly musical, the ocean
        takes the shore. Each wave's unconstrained
surface is thinned almost to transparency yet milky
        where the rims of giant floes displace silt.

A concert of algae, particles of minerals,
        microscopic plankton wisps—impermanently
forming foam. Ocean gathers reflected white cirrus,
        khaki sand, slate and quartz, wild rose bush gone to hips,

then saturates and streams through it all,
        steams over boundaries—those ledges
of land—and appropriates the large man
        who, with inexplicable optimism, faces the vast

expanse, scans the horizon for sails
        or a glimpse of seals. A girl nearly young enough
to remember her time in the womb darts away
        from the oncoming surf. A woman collects stones

rattled smooth by watery contact with knife-edged granite.
        We are all these people together in this opaque
immensity, our reflected faces and our forms
        drawn into sunless depths where we might

after eons of dreaming in oceans, learn
       the true nature of our close resemblances:
how we are the slow digestion of word into flesh,
       flesh into sustenance, our commonly uncommon

experiences settling into bottom muck to absorb
       into magma, metamorphose into inorganic matter
in time becoming a millionth particle
       of beauty. Today it seems to matter

that I am not you and yet the sea entices me
       to lose myself in all that is unseen, unknowable
because what I hear roaring, pitched to the tune
       of a hundred moist voices is this:

every song in any singular imagination is born from grains
       of *presence* distributed like seeds in a field, split
at those darkest hours in the most unseemly places
       when moisture enters through chinks worn into a person

by who knows which pain, what word. Whose dear voice?
       And so I sit here for hours intent to hear the healing
beginning of another pilgrimage, any conscious progress
       to inspire our next, necessary transformation.

Easter Sunrise: Halibut Point

We face the sun
we cannot see
because nothing
we have done
can stop the dawn
from arriving.

Morning comes in
the thin film between
ocean and heaven
where everything
is water, every-
thing is radiant.

Here in the rapture
of making room
for a new day
there is no place
for self-importance

And yet light advances
as if we, from shore,
had summoned all this
oscillating luminosity.

The wind wakes us,
waves brawl with stones
and gulls announce
the shattering
of shackles while we

stand here on a ledge
of rock at the end
of earth in the midst
of the tumult

and all around us
the bellowing surf
is fracturing brine into
the spectrum of your yearning.

Resolution At The Height Of Breath

In the liminal inhalation, to voice or keep silent remains dynamic
–
a choice.

Is it indecisive
or wise
to exhale
without sounding
an opinion?

Is this grief or is it joy
–
This gasp at the summit of awareness?.

The diminutive
pause after
exhalation will
always hold,
always,
its immanence
of death.

Despite the inevitable commitment of another violent injustice

there is still
this profusion of lilacs, these voluminous trees
spilling seeds.

Just listen to this righteous birdsong–*wheat wheat wheat,*
tree wick tree, blunder wonder, whittle whittle whittle whittle
cheery erie erie, and see see see see see. Tree.

I am, I know this now, to breathe.
To sing us into being.
See see see see see.

Dragonflies Wed In The Air

Japanese beetles destroyed my morning glories.
One day they copulated—iridescent beauties—
    on heart-shaped leaves.There is no pain, I thought,
    without brain to interpret constriction. So I pinched
them flat together in one ecstatic snap.
But what did I know of insect pleasure or torment? Dragonflies
    wed in the air. Imagine! Blue tandem soaring over water.
    Hitched, we'll call it. Appendages locked in grooves
and notches. His abdomen, the front of her thorax.
The two of them curl into a wheel, he the key to her lock
    until the urge to spawn calls her down to water to wash.
    She hovers, dips, scatters her eggs.
Eventually nymphs emerge. Some will evade
predatory fish to molt and molt again.
    Underwater. Becoming takes some time and even
    longer. Then someday in August, when vivid light

transforms the common marigold into something we pause
a long while to admire, nymphs will approach the film
    between worlds, pierce membrane separating water
    from sky. Maybe they break through
before a frog devours them. Maybe a couple—
(like you and I)—will elude death
    to climb on stone to split open to shed skin to suck air
    where wind or pelting rain could damage their wings

before the creatures ever fly. This is how I think about danger
about life, my love, and the meaning of us
    ever since you began to pause for a long while
    to admire your fixations. And now nearly daily
I trick fear by diversion when it seems I must
climb on stone to split open to shed skin to suck air
    because your mind is memory-mangled but you are
    still with me to wreathe us into what we are becoming.

As Though Your Chest Were Filling With Light
after Rumi

In the vast
prairie, the network
of myriad
species of insects,
pink-petaled
echinacea,
cranes and gold-
finch, decomposers,
gophers, grass,
rabbits, thistles—life
in all its
elemental forms—
you are not
all them, however
you notice
all of them. Be still
on the earth
and listen. She will
tell you who
you really are. Be.
Wait for the
illuminated
openness.
Become who you are.

After Survival

Our Souls Remember

My soul is striving to remember who I am, to make who I am
compatible with who I was born to be, to bring who I am into
synch with who I will be. – Steven Foster

Our emotional depths
    our lofty dreams
        imagine our veiled

essence embodied
    and wholly aware:
        clove on our tongues;

slender wheatgrass
    switching our shins;
        damp-wool-scented air;

the brook swollen
    from recent rain. Now
        listen higher than

the rush, notice
    a distant voice laughing
        itself into pleasure—

ah—freedom from fear.
 Our eyes enjoy a nickel-
  sized insect, blue

butterfly lilts ...Wild
 Lupine ... Purple Clover.
  Bee. Attentive, purpose-

full. Listen for
 the Word
  beneath the strung-out

words. Truth, not banter.
 And while leaning into
  our resilience may seem

as difficult as coaxing
 an orchestra to play
  Shostakovich's Symphony

No. 7, written with
 his heart's blood, perfectly,
  such concerted

listening requires
　　　only our attention.
　　　　　Hours, months, years.

A quiet lifetime
　　　practicing and re-
　　　　　membering that principled

practice is love,
　　　is lovely, *is*
　　　　　the perfect performance.

When The World Forgets To Listen
an improvisation on Rainer Maria Rilke's
Sonnets to Orpheus II (29)

Silence, now, you've come so far. Attune and tend
to the way your breath propagates spaciousness.
In the dark towers' rafters, you are
the bell chiming. Whatever overwhelms you

will become your nurturing power.
Go through your transformations.
Think of your most painful experience—
when the drink is bitter let it ferment into wine.

In this boundless night, you could become
mysticism at the crossroads of your senses,
be the meaning hidden behind strange encounters.

And when the world forgets to listen,
you will say to the mute earth: I flow.
To the rushing waters, declare: I am

Learning Kintsugi

Kintsugi: the Japanese art of repairing broken pottery with gold mortar; a philosophy of embracing our imperfections.

Because in every romance there will always
be a crack of trouble. Because
we contain many foxes who will fracture
us until we tame them by name.
Then they teach us to fill the chinks
desire makes with gold. Because
the fox named Shame is inseparable
from her mate and he remains
nameless until we recognize his name

is Rage. Both are creatures of moon,
shadows exquisite and easily broken.
Because pain refracts light only when
we look. Because poems are the ghosts
of stories too fragile to be spoken.
Because we can be broken and at
the same time whole because the art
of golden repair is the art of refusing
to hide the beautiful strength of our damage.

What Is There About Us Always (ii)

and now I

cleave to this belief

surely we

never love in vain

Acknowledgements

Thank you to editors, curators and staff of journals, newspapers, websites, and exhibits in which these poems first appeared, some in slightly different form:

Autumn Sky Poetry Daily: "What Is There About Us Always (i)" and "Sonnet To Negotiate Peace With Your Dementia"

Photowrite 2018 exhibit, Crossing Arts Alliance in Brainerd, MN: "Backlit Encounter"

Sauk Rapids Herald, "Nightfall With Perfumed Air"

LoveFirstUMC.org, a Trauma-Responsive Church, "Learning Kintsugi"

Rag Mag, "When She Stitched The Flag"

Publication of this book was made possible by the Central Minnesota Arts Board, thanks to funds provided through the McKnight Foundation. I am grateful to them, and to Christine Klocek-Lim and Lily Brutger for seeing, understanding, and exceeding what I was hoping to offer to readers through this little book. Thank you, Mara Faulkner, OSB for facilitating *Poetry At Work* in 2018 with your insightful, ground-breaking questions. Lyricality and this collection were seeded during our time together.

Thank you to my parents, brothers, sons, daughters-in-law and granddaughters, for almost never teasing me about my lifelong obsession with this strange little niche called poetry.

Dawn Bergacker, Susanne Ramm and Nancy Spitzack, your life-long friendship is as necessary as water, as restorative as tea. Hugs and Kisses to Amy Bergeron, Lynda Gradert, Linda Henrichs, Susan Thurston Hamerski and Kelly Travis for soul-sister magic and oodles of consistent support. Thank you to the enchanting Mettekor women, for singing me back home to my voice after bitter bereavement made me poetically and musically mute. To my compassionate team of caring listeners: Laureen Virnig, OSB; Michaela Hedican, OSB; Marie Hanauska, OblSB; Eunice Antony, OSB; Alison Hendley, OSB; The Rev. Dr. Shannon Michael Pater; Dr. Dorothee Ischler, OblSB; Dr. Almut Furchert, OblSB; Dr. Amanda Lovold, D.O.; Stephanie Hart; and to all the Sisters and Oblates of Saint Benedict's Monastery, especially Ann Marie Biermaier, OSB who offers a Studium scholar's office whenever I need the perfect blend of solitude and companionship, and the 1st Monday's Oblate Group—I never imagined my thriving would be supported by such an expansive and expanding safety net, woven from such varied and beautiful belonging.

Decades of gratitude to the Penchant Poets for early literary friendship and wise-woman counsel about life, love, parenting, friendship, and writing, with an extra measure to those who still show up every other week to read and respond to each other's poems—Karen Herseth Wee, Mary Moore Easter, Susan Thurston Hamerski, Marie Vogl Gery, and Karen Sandberg. Thank you Great River Poets and League of Minnesota Poets for being such kind-hearted companions for my journey. Your dedication to reading and writing makes my heart sing.

To the first readers of this collection, Bill Meissner, Paige Riehl, Kris Bigalk, KateLynn Hibbard, and Dennis Vogen, I am honored and made braver by your kind responses.

Thank you, thank you, thank you to the founding visionaries of Lyricality— Mickie Blenkush, Kate Buechler, Kelly Travis, and Cassidy Swanson. Without your imagination and commitment, Lyricality Press would not exist.

Most of all, I am thankful for my husband, Ken Rittmueller, whose love, support, and zany playfulness help me to appreciate daily moments of joy and serenity, even while we carry the increasing (and sometimes terrifying) losses that come with aging. Thank you, Bunky, for the beautiful, astonishing light of your being. I love you to infinity and beyond.

About the Author

Tracy Rittmueller is a crafter of poems, essays and stories, and the founding director of Lyricality, a Central Minnesota grass roots organization fostering the art of empathy through poetry and story. As a producer of cultural events and a teaching artist, she facilitates trauma-sensitive awareness in order to be deliberately inclusive, respectful of individual personhood, and increasingly aware of the ways language and authority are used within human relationships to give and take power.

She is a Benedictine Oblate (a professed associate) of Saint Benedict's Monastery in St. Joseph, Minnesota, dedicating her life to listening with the ear of her heart, and to offering the companionship of mutual empowerment to her diverse communities. She resides in a community of two with her Benedictine Oblate husband, Ken, in Sauk Rapids, Minnesota.

Her first collection, *Relearning The Lullaby,* was published by Heywood Press in 1993 as part of Northfield Women Poets *The Chapbook Series.*

Her website is TracyRittmueller.com

Lyricality Press

Lyricality Press is the book imprint of Lyricality, a grass roots collective of poets, writers, and artists dedicated to the principles and practices of diversity, equity, and inclusion. The press exists to magnify Minnesota's thriving, diverse literary arts scene by amplifying the voices of Minnesota poets and writers who may be considered (or consider themselves) outsiders to academic literary life due to income, language, health/ability, cultural values, education, age, and/or taste preferences.

Lyricality is a public charity recognized as tax-exempt by the IRS under Section 501(c)(3). To help sustain and grow our work, you can make a contribution online at **Lyricality.org/donate** or mail your check to

Lyricality
P.O. Box 172
Sauk Rapids, MN, 56379

Made in the USA
Monee, IL
30 January 2023

26756036R00039